𝓛iving 𝓗oly

In An Unholy World

KAREN M. PRESLEY

Anointed Press
PUBLISHERS

Cheltenham, Maryland
www.anointedpressgraphics.com/app_home.htm

LIVING HOLY IN AN UNHOLY WORLD

Unless otherwise indicated, all Scriptures' quotations are taken from The King James Version/ Amplified Parallel Edition. Copyright © 1995 by the Zondervan Corporation used by permission.

Scripture quotations marked AMP are from the King James Version/ Amplified Parallel Edition. Copyright © 1995 by the Zondervan Corporation, used by permission.

Scripture quotations marked NIV are from the NIV Rainbow Study Bible, (New International Version). Copyright © 1995 by Rainbow Studies, Inc. Used by permission.

ISBN 0-9789577-0-9
ISBN 978-0-9789577-0-4

Copyright © 2006
Karen M. Presley

This book was printed in the United States of America. All rights reserved under United States of America Copyright Law. This book or parts thereof may not be reproduced in any form or by any means – electronic, mechanical, photocopy, recording or otherwise – without prior written permission of the publisher, except as provided by United States of America copyright law.

A portion of proceeds are donated to:
Daughters of Zion Empowerment Center, Inc.
www.dzec.org

To purchase additional books:
www.anointedpresspublishers.com
or call 301-782-2285

Cover Design:
Anointed Press Graphics, Inc.
www.anointedpressgraphics.com
Copyright © 2006

Published by:
Anointed Press Publishers
(a subsidiary company of Anointed Press Graphics, Inc.)
11191 Crain Highway
Cheltenham, MD 20623
301-782-2285

Printed in the USA by Morris Publishing
3212 East Hwy 30
Kearney, NE 68847
1-800-650-7888

ACKNOWLEDGEMENTS

To my Lord, Jesus Christ, who is the Author and the Finisher of my faith. I thank God for the power of His grace in my life. Words cannot articulate how grateful I am for what He has done in me and through me.
I also thank God for my soon-to-be husband, whom God has prepared just for me and is an expression of His ultimate love for me.

To my pastors, Drs. Michael A. & Deloris R. Freeman
You have taught me the Word of faith and have been my example of what a man and woman of God should be in the earth.
I appreciate and honor you as a gift that God has placed in my life. I count it a privilege to call you my pastors, my covering and my spiritual parents in the faith.

I love you both!

DEDICATION

To my mother, Juanita B. Presley
Thank you for always believing in me.
Words cannot express my gratitude and appreciation
for your being there countless
times and for making a difference in my life.
I count it an honor and a privilege to call you my mother.

I love you & you are the best!

TABLE OF CONTENTS

Foreword by: Dr. Karyn C. Jones..7

Introduction..10

Chapter One
What is Holiness?..11

Chapter Two
Factoring in the Grace..19

Chapter Three
Deep Calling Deep..31

Chapter Four
You've Been Commissioned..45

Chapter Five
Evil is Present...57

Chapter Six
End Time Harvest..65

Chapter Seven
The Testimony...73

Prayer of Salvation..79

About the Author...80

FOREWORD

By: Dr. Karyn C. Jones
Executive Vice President/Administration
Faith Christian University and Schools

I know what it means to live an unholy or ungodly lifestyle. Attaching myself to people who are supposed to have my best interest at hand; only to discover there is no peace and no joy from within. Tormented by mirroring and comparing myself to what the world has defined as acceptable, I fell away from God. Afraid of being different, I accepted the hardship of the world, because my commitment to studying God's Word was only superficial; it had no depth, no meaning and no application, and yet I pretended that I was living the good life.

Because of the condition of my heart, I felt a void on the inside. I was always in and out of relationships, none of them fruitful. Many of us have based our relationships on how well a person has treated us. It is through these relationships that we determine how involved or intimate we will become. Even though we have committed ourselves totally and loved unconditionally as the flesh can, something happens and this relationship is severed. I began to live with the fear of being a failure, so I occupied myself with things, got involved in stuff to please me, as we all do; but, to no avail.

One day, after making a mess of everything, I began to do it God's way. My study habits changed, my commitment became stronger, and my love grew deeper for the things of him. I began to hunger and thirst like a chocoholic seeking for another bite. Then I realized it wasn't about me, but all about God. Here is where I found my true love, my unconditional love. God's love that kept no record, God's love that forgives and God's love that will last forever. This is why I believe this book entitled, Living Holy in an Unholy World, by Evangelist Karen M. Presley, is a book that will challenge and inspire every believer. Evangelist Presley has an anointing on her life because she too has allowed God to transform her from the inside out. She has allowed God to turn her life completely over to Him and to experience the outpouring of his grace and mercy.

    Living holy is a lifestyle that God has ordained from the beginning of time. God wanted a pure relationship with man. A relationship that is true and will breathe into the lives of others, in order for them to change. No man can live a spiritual life of holiness, if he does not know God. As you read this book, you will realize that the author has provoked your spirituality, and your thinking as well as your commitment to God.

    Oftentimes we are confused as to what holiness is, but, the Bible is clear when it says in 1Peter1:16, "Because it is written, Be ye holy; for I am holy". There is no confusion in this passage of scripture. Confusion comes when the flesh does not obey the spirit of God in you. Since man has the ability to choose, he toils with the idea of living holy or doing holy things. It is only when man stays connected to God that he realizes he can't do anything without him.

    Many Christians are living below their spiritual means. They have little appetite for the Word of God. They have doubt in the things of God. Their relationship with God is not where it should be, because they are looking over their shoulders to see what the world is doing. I believe this book was written to make us take inventory of ourselves, and to allow God to expose us for who we are.

Evangelist Karen M. Presley knows the price of the anointing. She knows that in order to trust God, you must have a true relationship with Him in order to hear His voice, before you can step out on his Word. When a believer is willing to throw everything away, that the world is offering, and turn his face towards God, for the sake of pleasing him, then you will know within yourself a change has been made. To live holy means also to be willing to endure the hardship that comes with the anointing, without compromising or complaining, but having the assurance that God is in control. As Christians, we know there are benefits when we live holy for God and every believer is entitled. Here are five benefits: [1] we have the love of God [2] we have access to him [3] we have power [4] we have vision [5] we have eternal life. With all these benefits, no wonder the world thinks we are mad.

This book is for the serious Christian who wants to live holy unto God. This book is also for the Christian, who don't care if they are being talked about, lied about, or even being misused. This book is for the men and women who are ready to give up the self-pleasures of this world, in order to gain their rightful place with God.

My prayer to every reader is that you will not only enjoy this book, but you will read it as a guide to express, experience and explore all the things God has done for you and through you, so you can be a witness to others as a testimony of living holy.

INTRODUCTION

I have heard all my life that I was going to write a book. In February 2006, God spoke to me, "that now was the time to write the book". A week later, God gave me the title "Living Holy in an Unholy World."

This book was inspired by God, to enable the believer to overcome world chaos in the last days and experience the victory that belongs to the believer, in spite of the negative reports. The Bible says that, in the last days there will be wars and rumors of wars; nations will rise against nations, there will be an increase of pestilence, famine and earthquakes in divers places; and because of the iniquity that is on the earth, the love of many will grow cold. However beloved, God said that these things must take place on the earth, but the end is not yet. (Matthew 24)

Living Holy in an Unholy World will show you that, although evil is present, greater is He that lives in you than he that lives in the world; greater in power, greater in might, greater in love. Peace and joy dwells in you beloved and God is looking for believers who will dare to trust Him in spite of what they hear or see.

So, as you read this book, allow the Spirit of God to permeate your thinking and your heart, to bring you into the full understanding of who you are and what He wants to do through you in these end times. It's never too late! Whether you are a new Christian or a seasoned saint, God is looking to do more through you!

Chapter 1

WHAT IS HOLINESS?

"*But as he which hath called you is holy, so be ye holy in all manner of conversation; Because it is written, Be ye holy, for I am holy.*" 1 Peter 1:15, 16

In the light of this scripture, we were commanded to live holy; however, in order to do that we must do away with all the misconceptions of what society has called "holiness".

Holiness does not mean that women must wear a hat on their head or no make-up on their faces, nor does it mean that women must wear skirts to there ankles. Holiness does not mean that you must wear white every day, nor does it mean that you must be in the house before it gets dark. Holiness is not how many times you can say "Praise the Lord" or "I'm Blessed" throughout the day, nor is it how many bumper stickers you have on your car that says "I'm a Christian." Holiness simply is having one's life yielded to God. In other words, you have made yourself pliable in the Hand of God. It doesn't mean you are perfect nor does it mean you have arrived. It is simply a life that is obedient to God.

I'm reminded of a song writer's lyrics that say, "Holiness is what He wants from us, so take my heart and mold it, take my mind and transform it, and take my will and conform it… to yours oh Lord." When we daily give God our heart, mind and will, we are relinquishing our self to God, so we can be processed into a vessel of holiness. Process denotes a course of action or procedures taking place, that will bring us into another state or a different disposition. God has to process our old mentality, our old way of doing things, and, our old way of functioning through the every day dealings of God in our lives. We are conformed into God's image, though His dealing in our lives.

Righteousness is a gift you received when you accepted Jesus Christ as Lord; however, holiness requires obedience to the will of God. Romans 12:1 (amp) says,

"I appeal to you therefore, brethren, and beg of you in view of [all] the mercies of God, to make a decisive dedication of your bodies [presenting all your members and faculties] as a living sacrifice, holy (devoted, consecrated) and well pleasing to God, which is your reasonable (rational, intelligent) service and spiritual worship."

Paul wasn't talking to the unsaved for he said "brethren", that meant he was talking to the church. He was begging the church to live holy before God and said that it was an act of worship. It is our responsibility to present our members unto God. God says that He sees it as an act of our will. The Bible further tells us that we are to reckon ourselves dead to sin and we're not to yield our members as instruments of unrighteousness unto sin, but yielding ourselves unto God. (Romans 6:11-13) A life of holiness requires our obedience and our willingness to God's Word and presence in our lives. Take my heart, my mind and my will says that I recognize that I am nothing without God and I need Him in my life. I recognize His supremacy, authority and sovereignty in my life.

In the book of Luke chapter 10, we see an account with Martha and Mary and how Martha was busy working and cumbered about with much serving, but Mary was at the feet of Jesus listening to His Words. The Bible says, that it was Mary who had chosen the good part, for Jesus said it was needful; not delightful, not satisfying but NEEDFUL. Jesus knew that it was crucial to the life of a believer to sup with Him and to spend time in His presence. In order to be an effective witness on the earth, the believer would need to be sensitive to the voice of God. As a child of God, it is needful that we develop a relationship with God through His Word and through prayer. Beloved, stop fighting and allow Him to sit on the throne of your heart to bring you into this life called "holiness", for it has great rewards.

RENDERING YOUR HEART

Often times we find ourselves very busy with church responsibilities, auxiliaries, different church services and meetings that we forget to spend time with the God of the church. The Bible tells us that our obedience is better than sacrifice (1 Samuel 15:22). Why, because regardless of what we do for God and in the name of God, it doesn't mean anything if we are not obeying God. In the book of Revelations chapter 2, Jesus tells the church of Ephesus that He knows about their works and the fact that they have labored for His name sake; however, one account He had against this church was that they left their first love. They got so caught up in all the activities of the church that they weren't spending any time with the Lord. God is to be first and foremost the center of everything we do. He is the reason why we come to church and He should be the center of our worship. We must find and maintain balance in our relationship with God as well as our service that we render unto God.

Isaiah 29:13 says,

"Wherefore the Lord said, forasmuch as this people draw near me with their mouth and with their lips do honor me, but have removed their heart far from me and their fear toward me is taught by the precept of men."

That means men have learned by repetition without any thought as to the meaning. We come to church and we have learned church. God says He needs our heart connected to everything we do. I like to give the example of bullets inside of a gun. The gun is only a dangerous weapon if it is loaded with bullets. The bullets are only effective if they have gun powder in them. So, in order for the gun to be effective, it must have all of the components. In the same manner, power is released in our lives, when our heart is connected to what we do. Whether we are praying, praise and worship, serving in church, tithing, or just coming to attend church service, our heart must be connected to God.

God is only obligated to move on our behalf, and show Himself strong in our your heart, and don't allow it to become contaminated with the junk that's in this world. Hebrews 12:1, tells us to lay aside every weight, every distraction, and every obstacle that so easily besets you. We've been commanded to run this race with faith and patience; knowing that the Author and Finisher of our faith will bring to pass every promise in our lives, as long as we hold onto the Word of God.

God is requiring our hearts first and foremost unto Him and He says when you turn unto Him with fasting, removing every hindrance until your broken fellowship is restored, He will deliver you from that which the enemy has stolen. God promised that He will restore to you the years that the locust and the cankerworm and the caterpillar and the palmerworm have eaten. (Joel 2:23)

What that means is that all the years that the enemy had robbed you of your health, your peace of mind, your joy, your self-worth, your self-esteem, your childhood, God said, He is going to restore, give back and return to the former, everything the enemy has stolen. God promised that when it was all said and done, He would be in the midst of thee and His people shall not be ashamed. Child of God, it starts with giving your heart completely to God!

A LIFE THAT'S PLIABLE

Jeremiah 18:6 says,

"O house of Israel, cannot I do with you as this potter? Saith the Lord, Behold, as the clay is in the potter's hand, so are ye in mine hand, O house of Israel."

In this chapter, we see the heart of God towards His people and how He desires for us to be in His hand. The Word of the Lord came to the prophet Jeremiah, to go to the potter house and their God would speak to him concerning Israel. God says, the same way the clay is in the hands of the potter, we are to be in the hand of God.

Holiness is having a life that is pliable and moldable in the hand of the Almighty, All-Loving, and All-Knowing God who created us in His image. God is the Master Architect of our vessels; He knows the blue print that will bring us into the fullness of our destiny and purpose. When the potter sees that a vessel is marred, he decides to make it again. In the same way, God says, I have seen every injustice in your life that caused you to be where you are today.

Child of God, you must understand that even though we were created in the image of God, our experiences, upbringing, environment, negative words and the things we lacked growing up, shape who we are today. There are many factors in our lives that determine how we see things, how we respond or react and how we relate to issues and people.

You must know that the devil comes to rob, steal and destroy because he does not want you to experience who you really are in Christ. The devil's tactic is to keep you from everything that belongs to you, for he knows the potential and treasure that lies in you. He wants to leave you emotionally broken and fragmented, so you will not have the confidence to walk in what God pre-ordained. That is why his strategies keep the believer in a place of bondage.

God is determined to bring you into your destiny, but it comes through a life of holiness. Walking in holiness is allowing God to fix every area of your life, which ultimately makes you into the vessel that He originally intended for you to be. Jeremiah 17:9,10 says,

"The heart is deceitful above all things, and desperately wicked; who can know it? I the Lord search the heart, I try the reins, even to give every man according to his ways, and according to the fruit of his doings."

When we become pliable in the hand of God, we are recognizing His loving guidance and direction in our lives. We recognize and permit His corrections in our daily goings and we make ourselves available to the Spirit of God, for Him to show us the areas in our lives that need to be dealt with. Holiness is growing up and out of a life of carnality; recognizing that there is a God and going to church to fulfill your sense of duty. Holiness is allowing God into your daily affairs and allowing His hand to guide and correct you, which will ultimately bring you into your rightful place as sons of God.

The Bible says that all of creation is waiting for the sons of God to manifest. (Romans 8) That means, it is time for the body of Christ to grow up into their rightful positions. We should be taking our places as kings in the earth, exercising our authority and taking dominion in the places that God has strategically placed us.

We see an awesome lesson from Jesus in the book of John chapter 15, about the branches remaining in the vine and how the vinedresser dresses or keeps it. We are the branch, Jesus is the vine and the branch has no life in itself. All of its nourishments and source of supply come from the vine, for without it the branch would be dead. Likewise, our responsibility is to abide, remain and stay connected in Jesus through, and by, fellowshipping with the Word of God, prayer and communion with the Holy Spirit.

God's responsibility as our Vinedresser is to watch over, to prune, and correct us so we might produce more fruit and bring about the deep hidden treasures that lie in us. God desires for us to produce and manifest the very thing that He placed on the inside of us, so that He might be glorified on the earth.

Holiness is about growing into maturity and allowing God's loving hand, to daily direct and instruct us into the way of truth for our lives. God loves you so much and He desires that you walk in everything He had purposed for you. Child of God, before you were born, before your mother met your father, you were already in the mind of God, full of potential, full of purpose, full of destiny, assignments, hopes and dreams. Psalms 139:16 (amp) says,

> *"Your eyes saw my unformed substance, and in Your book all the days [of my life] were written before ever they took shape, when as yet there was none of them."*

God has already walked out your steps, for He declares the end from the beginning. (Isaiah 46:10) He's the Alpha and Omega, the First and Last, the Beginning and End and everything in between. Your loving Daddy is waiting for you to grow up and step into the thing that rightfully belongs to you and that comes through a life of holiness. I encourage you, as you continue to read this book, allow God to speak to the different areas in your life that need adjusting, so He can bring you into your inheritance, which is a better quality of life that He has planned for you.

Chapter 2

FACTORING IN THE GRACE

Have you ever tried to fulfill God's instructions found in His Word, in your own ability? Do you love the Lord, but find yourself not being able to do the thing that He's requiring of you? Do you find yourself saying what Paul said in Romans chapter 7,

"I do what I know not to do and I don't do what I know to do?"

So many times, we forget that God has given us His grace to help us fulfill His Word in our lives. What is grace? Grace is unmerited favor. But, my Pastor defines grace as, God's divine ability, power and enablement on our behalf so we might have, be, and do all that God said we can have, be and do. God's Word is His covenant and it's filled with promises, commandments, and consequences. Beloved, God would never tell us to keep His Word and not give us the ability to do it. He is an All-Loving God, and He desires us not to fail. Beloved, God has a plan for you, not of evil but good and He wants to bring you into your expectant end. (Jeremiah 29:11) God is waiting for us to lean on Him, expecting Him, by faith, to fulfill His Word in our lives. Obeying Holy Spirit's daily instructions, by walking out the things that that are impressed upon our hearts to do.

Ephesians 2:8 says,

"For by grace are we saved thru faith and that not of yourselves, it is the gift of God."

God's grace is a gift that He has given to the believer. You do not have to work for it; there isn't a ten step program to get it – IT'S FREE! Hallelujah! God's gift to us is His ability and enablement working in our lives so we might fulfill what He ordained for us before the foundation of the world.

There was a season in my life that I knew God wanted me to get up in the morning and spend time with Him. Child of God, it was a struggle for me to get up in the morning because I am not a morning person. To be honest with you, I love my bed and I love sleep; however, I love God more. So, I used to confess, "God I thank you that I'm going to see more of you today." One day after I said that, God so politely said, "Karen, you are the one who is going to make that happen." I said, "What do you mean?" God said, "When I wake you up in the morning to pray, DO IT!" Right there, I confessed to God that I was not a morning person, but if you give me the grace to get up, I'll get up. From that moment on, God has given me His ability, which is His grace to get up and spend time with Him in the morning. Praise God! His grace is available to all of us. He is just waiting for us to put a demand on it.

One day a long time ago, I had an encounter with the Lord and He spoke to me, "you looked like a gentle flower growing in grace… the grace of God was all over me and God had prepared me and equipped me to do what God had called me to do. So walk in what God called me to do boldly." Child of God, at that time I didn't really know what that meant and I definitely didn't know the impact of that word in my life. But, after ten years of walking with God, I see the magnitude of that prophetic Word in my life.

When I look back over the different seasons in my life and the different places I found myself, truly it was God's grace that enabled me to do the different tasks that were set before me. I know that I could not have obtained or achieved some of the accolades that I achieved on different jobs, if it wasn't for His grace and His anointing on my life. But, I knew that every job He had placed me on was for a purpose.

Beloved, as I stated earlier, God has a plan for your life and it is a plan of good and not of evil, to bring you into your destiny. He already knew that in and of yourself, you could not walk this walk alone; but, He said that He has equipped you with everything you needed, to be the success that He created you to be. He already knew about your frailties, weaknesses, inconsistencies, your inabilities and sin that so easily besets you, but 1 Corinthians 1:27, tells us,

"God has chosen the foolish things of the world to confound the wise and God has chosen the weak things of the world to confound the things which are mighty."

Why? -- So no flesh would glory in His presence. If you could make it happen on your own, then you wouldn't give God the credit that belongs to Him. Beloved, God on purpose picked you. He meant for you to be limited, you were supposed to be treated less than your prophecy; because His plan was that He was gonna show up and out in your life.

God's grace is all over you, because He is enabling you by His grace to be what He had pre-ordained you to be. Beloved, before you came out of your mother's womb, He already knew you and set you apart for His glory. (Jeremiah 1:5)

ABIDING IN THE VINE

John 15:4-5 says,

"Abide in me, and I in you. As the branch cannot bear fruit of itself, except it abide in the vine; no more can ye, except ye abide in me. I am the vine, ye are the branches: He that abide in me and I in him, the same bringeth forth much fruit; for without me ye can do nothing."

Beloved, Jesus so clearly states that our job as Christians is to abide, remain and stay connected with Him through His Word and in prayer. I've said this before, but, a branch in itself has no life in it and the Bible says that we are the branches and Jesus is the vine. The source of the branches' supply and nourishment comes through the vine. Just like the branch cannot live without the vine, child of God, you must know that you cannot live without God's Word.

Our daily relationship with the Lord Jesus Christ is vital to our spiritual maturity. The Bible says that, as we abide in Him and His Word abides in us, that mean it's alive and operable; then we'll bring forth much fruit in our lives. The fruit of God is displaying the nature and character of God in our lives. God is love and everything we do must be motivated by His love.

It is imperative that we bring forth the fruit of God in our lives that He might be glorified in the earth. As we allow God's Word to start producing in us, God will then prune the areas that are producing, so that more fruit, and then much fruit might spring forth and abound in our lives.

It is time that Christians become spiritually minded and not carnally minded. As we continue to abide in daily fellowship with the presence of God, it will cause us to be more sensitive and in tune to the Spirit of God. We must become people who are kingdom-minded so God would begin to demonstrate His power through us in a greater measure. Paul said in Galatians 2:21,

"I do not frustrate the grace of God, for if righteousness comes by the law, then Christ is dead in vain."

Paul knew first hand that if he was going to be successful on his journey with the Lord, that it wasn't going to be about what he could make happen. But, it was going to take him relying on God's grace and abiding in His presence that caused Paul to be great in the Kingdom of God. Paul was an ex-religious ruler who terrorized Christians and orchestrated the killing of them. So, when God called him, he also anointed and equipped him to do a mighty work for Him. Paul said, "I am what I am, only by the grace of God." Paul knew that it wasn't by his might and strength that he was able to do great things, but he constantly relied on the grace of God that enabled him to be great in God's kingdom.

We must follow that same example that Paul set and rely on God's grace to carry us daily. Remember the grace of God is the power of God that enables us to do what we can't do on our own. God's grace is a gift that has been extended to every believer, not just to accomplish the call on our lives, but to help us in our every day living.

There is a grace to be a parent, secretary, bus driver, CEO of a company, entrepreneur, construction worker, salesperson, a student, athlete, entertainer or whatever your assignment is. God has given you the grace to be the best at whatever you have been called to be. But, just like Paul, we can't frustrate the grace of God by trying to do things on our own; we must abide in the vine through prayer and fellowshipping with His Word. This is how God is going to show Himself strong and mighty in the earth.

Finally, I want to tell you that God's grace is ours for the asking. One Saturday I remember having so much to do. I woke up really overwhelmed in my mind with the many chores on my things-to-do list. I knew I only had that Saturday to do them. I was really tired and a part of me just wanted to sleep all day but, because of my tremendously busy schedule, I had to do them that day. I got out of the bed around 11:00 a.m. and asked God for His grace to help me get everything done that I needed to get done.

Well, let me tell you that God's grace is real and it enabled me to do everything I needed that day. I washed four loads of clothes, cleaned both bathrooms, vacuumed my floor, washed dishes, paid my bills, went grocery shopping, went to the post office, got my car washed, fixed dinner and worked on my book. The best part about all of this was that God's grace not only enabled me to accomplish this, but I wasn't even tired. Thank God for His grace! He wants to show out in our lives so that we might be a testimony in the earth of His faithfulness and His daily provision to His children.

HOLY SPIRIT'S ROLE

Jesus not only reconciled us back to the Father, but He introduced us to the Holy Spirit. John 14:16,17 says,

"And I will pray the Father and he shall give you another Comforter, that he may abide with you for ever. Even the Spirit of truth; whom

the world cannot receive, because it seeth him not, neither knoweth him: but ye know him; for he dwelleth with you and shall be in you."

(v. 26), "But the Comforter, which is the Holy Ghost whom the Father will send in my name, he shall teach you all things, and bring all things to your remembrance, whatsoever I have said unto you."

The greatest gift the believer should cherish is the precious Holy Spirit that dwells on the inside of every person who has made Jesus Christ, the Lord of their lives.

I remember one day, back in the year 1995, I attended a seminar called, "**The School of the Holy Spirit**." This seminar emphatically changed my life. It was at this two day seminar that I learned how to develop a relationship with Holy Spirit. Child of God, knowing the Holy Spirit daily is what is going to take us from being a carnally minded Christian to a spiritually minded Christian.

God needs us to mature, so we might be fit for the master's use. It is only going to come by knowing the Holy Spirit and His role in our lives. Spending time in the presence of God is the key to developing this relationship with Holy Spirit.

Many times we pray on the run or we don't sit still in God's presence and allow Him to minister to us. Sitting still, in the presence of God, sharpens your inner man and causes you to be more in tune to His voice. It's not about if you hear an audible voice, but knowing that you are becoming more aware and sensitive to His unctions and promptings and leading in your everyday living.

The Bible says in John 10:27,

"My sheep hear my voice, and I know them, and they follow me."

It is imperative that believers know the voice of God just like the Word of God. Also, acknowledging the Holy Spirit's help throughout the day on daily decisions will help you to know Him daily. When you acknowledge the Holy Spirit to assist you, help you, teach you, give you counsel or wisdom or answers to anything that arises in your day, no matter how small or big, grace is made available to bring forth that which you need. Proverbs 3:5-6 says,

"Trust in the Lord with all thine heart; and lean not unto thine own understanding. In all your ways acknowledge him and he shall direct thy path."

It is the will of God that you develop a relationship with Holy Spirit, the One who reveals to you what the Father is speaking concerning you. The Bible says, that it is the Holy Spirit who knows the heart and mind and the will of God concerning your life, for He is the One who searches the deep things of God. (1 Corinthians 2:10) It is essential to the life of the believer that if we are going to be what God called us to be and, have what God called us to have, and do what God called us to do, it is going to come by knowing the Holy Spirit daily.

Holy Spirit is the One who will walk us into everything that belongs to us. Child of God, your Father desires for you to walk in His truth concerning who you are and walk in the freedom from your past and wholeness in every area of your life. By communing with Holy Spirit, we begin to experience the fullness of His presence operating in our lives.

The Spirit of God always bares witness with the Word of God, for He cannot speak of Himself but only what He hears the Father speaketh in heaven. (1 John 5:7) The Holy Spirit is here to aide, assist, and help us in our daily lives. We are not alone to fend for ourselves; God has given the believer Himself to enable us to be victorious in the earth. The Bible says that power and might are in His hands (Exodus 32:11) and He inhabits the praises of His people. (Psalms 22:3)

When we get into the presence of God and start loving up on Him by thanking Him and exalting Him and telling Him how great He is, then God begins to manifest His presence; that is why we shouldn't be so quick to pray and praise, but learn to discipline ourselves to sit still and wait on God. When God manifests His presence, He begins to rub on, smear on, paint on us His anointing and power in our lives. Child of God, your Father never comes empty handed, because in His hand is power, might blessings, and when God shows up, He comes to smear on you all of Himself. God will rub on you His ability that will enable you to do what it is you need to do, in whatever arena you find yourself in.

No longer shall you fall subject to the voice of insecurity, inability or inadequacy, because you've been in the presence of the Almighty God and allowed Him to smear you with His anointing. It's the anointing that causes you to have sweatless victory in your life; no stress, strain or struggle.

The anointing is available because it is the personality of the Holy Ghost and the Holy Ghost lives in you. 1 John 2 says,

"But the anointing which ye have received of him abideth in you, and ye need not that any man teach you; but as the same anointing teacheth you of all things, and is truth and is no lie, and even as it hath taught you, ye shall abide in him."

Child of God, you are equipped with the power of God that teaches you all things. That's why, as believer, we don't have to struggle with trying to accomplish daily tasks, in our own ability, nor do we need to call on people to help us with things we don't know how to do. The Bible says, we have this anointing that teaches us all things. (1 John 2:27) That's not just spiritual things, but natural things as well. Things we need to know in our daily living. Sometimes we find ourselves waiting for people to help us, and if they are busy, we become in limbo waiting for people. Factoring in the grace, means acknowledging God and allowing Him to show forth His ability, power and goodness in our lives. Developing a relationship with Holy Spirit is the key to our success and walking into all the benefits that Jesus died for. There is a price to pay, my friend, but it is well worth it when you see the results of walking and being in tune with Holy Spirit.

Except for the three years that I was married, I lived with my mother all my life, because I never thought I could make it on my own. One day, at the age of 35, God said, "it is time to move out on my own, and He was going to grow me up." You see stuff like taking care of household items and everything else was all new to me. When I moved into my house simultaneously I started taking a semester at college and I was maintaining my job and my home-based business. So, as you see, there was a lot going on at the same time. So many decisions needed to be made, accounts to open as it relates to my house and stuff to put together. I felt like I went from two responsibilities to ten, overnight! But, in that time, God's grace enabled me to do everything I needed to do on a daily basis.

By God's grace, He enabled me to balance out the many tasks that were set before me. Even my mother was amazed at how it seemed like I grew up overnight, because for so long she did everything. Remember, I thought I couldn't make it on my own so it wasn't until I moved out that His grace carried me throughout that season to do what I couldn't do in my own ability.

Even as it relates to taking care of the yard work, everything was on me because I had no mother to lean on. There are a lot of responsibilities to maintaining head of household, business, job, ministry and school. I thank God for His grace because I could not have made it without it. And, the same way that God enabled me to prevail, through and by the power of His grace, is the same way God wants you to prevail – by His grace.

God is obligated to take care of you and equip you with His grace, when you step out and obey His written and rhema (spoken) Word for your life. Wherever you are today, in your walk with the Lord, trust God to carry you through victoriously, for He cares for you and He's calling you into a deeper relationship with Him.

THE LEVEL OF OUR THINKING, ACTING AND OPERATING THAT GOT YOU TO WHERE YOU ARE RIGHT NOW --WILL NOT TAKE YOU TO WHERE IT IS THAT GOD WANTS YOU TO BE

Chapter 3

DEEP CALLING DEEP

P salms 42:1-2 (NIV) says,

"As the deer pants for streams of water, so my soul pants for you, O God. My soul thirst for God, for the living God. When can I go and meet with God?

(v 7-8), Deep calls to deep in the roar of your waterfalls; all your waves and breakers have swept over me. By day the Lord directs his love, at night his song is with me— a prayer to the God of my life."

In order to get the significance of what the psalm writer is saying, we must learn about the life of a deer. The psalmist compares his yearning for God to the longing that a deer has for water. The deer's life is sustained by water, forms a simile for our soul's need and thirst for the living God. God is a Spirit and we were created in the likeness of God, for it is our spirit that is just like God. Our soul consists of our mind, emotions and will, so when the psalmist said that his soul was yearning for the living God, he was saying that everything in him needed to be in the presence of the Almighty God, the One who created him.

In Psalms 16, we find that in the presence of God, there is fullness of joy. He also recognizes his need for a personal relationship with a living God. As we draw nigh unto God, He will draw nigh unto us. God desires not only that you receive His son Jesus as the propitiator for your sins, but also a relationship with your Daddy, who loves you. He loved us so much that while we were still in our sin, He sent His only begotten son Jesus to die on the cross.

Ephesians 2:13,14 (amp) says,

"But now in Christ Jesus, you who once were [so] far away, through (by ,in) the blood of Christ have been brought near. For He is [Himself] our peace (our bond of unity and harmony), He has made us both [Jew and Gentile] one [body] and has broken down (destroyed, abolished) the hostile dividing wall between us."

Beloved, there is no longer a barrier between you and your Father, for Jesus has abolished the wall. Your Heavenly Father is calling you into a personal relationship and intimacy with Him, not just to sit in church and fulfill an obligation. Deep calling deep is a call to go pass the realm of your carnal mind into the depth of your spirit, to discover the greatness of God's glory in your life. We must pursue God with the same intensity that the deer pursues water and not get relaxed or religious (traditional).

Paul also discovered this need and desire to know and become acquainted with God through the Lord Jesus Christ.

Philippians 3:8,10 (amp)

"Yes, furthermore, I count everything as loss compared to the possession of the priceless privilege (the overwhelming preciousness, the surpassing worth and supreme advantage) of knowing Christ Jesus my Lord and of progressively becoming more deeply and intimately acquainted with Him [of perceiving and recognizing and understanding Him more fully and clearly]. For His sake I have lost everything and consider it all to be mere rubbish (refuse, dregs), in order that I may win (gain) Christ (the Anointed One)

(v.10) [For my determined purpose is] that I may know Him [that I may progressively become more deeply and intimately acquainted with Him, perceiving and recognizing and understanding the wonders of His Person more strongly and more clearly] and that I may in that same way come to know the power out flowing from His resurrection [which it exerts over believers] and that I may so share His sufferings as to be continually transformed [in spirit into His likeness even] to His death, [in the hope]."

Wow, this is powerful! Paul's desire was to count or consider everything in his life that he had previously accomplished but rubbish and gone for the sake of the Anointed One and His Anointing. As I stated earlier, Paul, who was an ex-religious ruler, who had clout, status and was used to an entourage, said whatever he had or whatever he was used to or whatever he use to do, he counted it all but gone.

He threw it all away for the sake of knowing and being intimate with the Anointed One and His Anointing. His only purpose now was to share in Christ's suffering by dying to this flesh daily so that he might know and experience the power of His resurrection, the power of His victory in his life. The power to overcome every area of our lives is available to us.

We too must follow Paul's example by surrendering and depositing our lives in Christ, so He might be fully formed in us. You might be asking, what does it mean to be fully formed? Child of God, when you received Jesus as Lord of your life, the Spirit of God came to live on the inside of you. But, how much of God you allow to flow through you depends on your obedience to Him. Dying to the flesh is not always easy, because our flesh loves to take matters in it's own hands. Dying to the flesh means, not your will, but God's will be done in your life. In every situation that arises in your life and that's not comfortable.

David said in Psalms 27,

"One thing have I desired of the Lord, that will I seek after; that I may dwell in the house of the Lord all the days of my life, to behold the beauty of the Lord and to inquire in his temple."

I often say that David was not absent of problems, but in spite of his success in leading Israel in many of victories over other nations, David knew the secret of his success was spending time in the presence of God. David also had clout, status and an entourage surrounding him. But, he knew he needed God in his life and he only had one desire and that was to pursue the Almighty and Sovereign God. David wasn't trying to chase his success nor did he get stuck in a routine of religion, but his desire was to keep his relationship fresh with the living God who turned him from a shepherd boy into a mighty warrior that led the Nation of Israel into many victories.

David said there was ONE thing he desired and that was to dwell in the house of the Lord. David had experienced all of the goodness and fullness that comes with spending time with God. He equated that there was no comparison on earth to being with God. David was a shepherd boy whose duties were tending to the sheep. He had plenty of time to be alone with God. When God was looking for another king to replace Saul, David had the heart of God, through his worship. David was overlooked by man, but was brought from behind the scene to the center stage because of his relationship with God.

In conclusion, we need to imitate the examples that we have before us in the Word by worshipping God in the Spirit, rejoicing in Christ Jesus and having no confidence in our flesh. (Philippians 3:3) This is how we mature in Christ so we might display His glory in our lives.

RELATIONSHIP vs. RELIGION

"Now when these things were thus ordained, the priests went always into the first tabernacle, accomplishing the service of God. But into the second went the high priest alone once every year, not without blood, which he offered for himself and for the errors of the people. The Holy Ghost this signifying, that the way into the holiest of all was not yet made manifest, while as the first tabernacle was yet standing." (Hebrews 9:6-8)

The book of Exodus is where it is described in detail that Israel's worship consisted of blood sacrifices. Due to sin, God instituted the Tabernacle because He desired to dwell among His people; therefore, He implemented blood sacrifices. The Bible says that the life of a thing is in the blood; (Leviticus 17:11) therefore, blood had to be shed for the redemption of sins. (Ephesians 1:7)

God was very specific when He spoke with Moses as to the materials, the measurements and dimensions of the outer court, the inner court and the Most Holy Place, as well as the furniture that would be in each section. God even instructed Moses that the priesthood would preside over the nation's religious life. The priests were to also minister in the tabernacle in a variety of ways. The Tabernacle would be the place where God would meet the children of Israel. God's glory was manifested in the Most Holy Place. The priest was instructed that they had to bring an acceptable offering before God and each offering had a meaning and indicated something to God.

For example, the burnt offerings and fellowship offerings would result in His name being honored and their lives being blessed. God was very precise, He told them that it had to be a specific male animal and without blemish. God wasn't taking any old thing; He said I require your best. After they presented to God their offering and went through the routine that was instituted by God, the fire of God would consume their offering. After that, the priest would go to the laver to wash and proceed to the Holy Place to continue in worship unto God.

This would be their routine for the entire time that Israel wandered in the wilderness under the leadership of Moses. They would pack up when God said it was time to move and stop at their next designation. God would direct them by a pillar of cloud by day and a pillar of fire by night. It was a ceremony that, when followed precisely, God would manifest His presence.

After Moses came back from on top of Mt. Sinai with the regulations, commandments and laws that God set to govern the children of Israel, a ceremony to ratify the covenant was performed. This ceremony consisted of blood sprinkled on the altar of burnt offerings as well as Israel symbolizing that they would obey the commands, regulations and laws. (Exodus 24-31)

Well, needless to say, the church no longer has to worship God through blood sacrifices. What the blood of goats and calves could not do, Jesus, who died on our behalf, shed His own blood, entered into the holy place and obtained eternal redemption for us. (Hebrews 9:12) Because of Jesus Christ, we have a new covenant, a better covenant with better promises.

Because of Jesus Christ's death, burial and resurrection, the veil in the temple was rent in two, symbolizing that we no longer had to go through a priest, but we could come boldly before the throne of grace. God said in the book of Jeremiah, that the day would come when He would make a new covenant with the house of Israel and with the house of Judah. But, He said it wouldn't be according to the covenant that He made with their fathers in the days of the wilderness, but how God would make a new covenant by putting His law in their inward parts and write it in their hearts, and He would be their God and they would be His people. (Jeremiah 31:31-33) Child of God, please understand that God has designed us for purpose and to fellowship with Him, through His son Jesus Christ. The way has been made available, the path is straight, the King's scepter is extended and He is beckoning you to come unto Him for God desires relationship with you.

When Jesus came on the scene, He only spoke of what He heard the Father say. Jesus was the expressed image of the Father, He was the Word made flesh that dwelt among us. (John 1:14) Jesus came not to condemn man by the law, but to preach the good news of the Gospel that He saves, delivers, heals, sets free and to reveal the Father unto many. That is why God declared whosoever received Jesus received the Father.

The Bibles says in Mark 7:6-9,

"He answered and said unto them, Well hath Esaias prophesied of you hypocrites, as it is written, This people honoureth me with their lips, but their hearts is far from me. Howbeit in vain do they worship me, teaching for doctrines the commandments of men. For laying

aside the commandment of God, ye hold the tradition of men as the washing of pots and cups: and many other such like things ye do. And he said unto them, Full well ye reject the commandment of God, that ye may keep your own tradition."

Jesus was constantly challenged by the Pharisees and the Sadducees concerning His teaching. Jesus said, they were hypocrites because they confessed one thing but did another. They preached the Word to others but yet didn't live the Word. That is why they never recognized Jesus as the Messiah, the Word made flesh, the One who came in the volume of the book.

Even today we see the same thing in the church. So many people hold onto their traditions and their customs, and their way of doing things, making the power and the Word of God of no effect in their lives. Jesus said, that He was the fulfillment of the law and how the church entered into a dispensation of grace when He came on the scene. In Matthew 11:25, Jesus was thanking God because He hid His truth from those who claimed to be wise and prudent, but to the babes, He revealed His truth. This is an overall principal with God, as we become like little children before God, not confessing to have our own wisdom but leaning on God in everything we do, He said that is the person that I will reveal my wisdom and counsel unto.

God is looking for our dependency on Him and that comes through relationship and daily communing with the Father. Even the staff that Moses carried, when he led the children of Israel out of Egypt and through the wilderness, symbolized his constant dependency and trust in God. The staff also symbolized Moses' need for God's direction in his life in leading the children of Israel. Moses never became familiar or complacent, even though they wandered around the wilderness for forty years. His dependency on God was just as fresh when he was first called forty years ago.

We come into the church and become stagnant and religious, knowing the order of church, but never getting to know the God of the church. We know the church lingo and we have bumper stickers indicating that we are Christians; however, we never fully surrendered all. The body of Christ should always be moving forward in the things of God.

After salvation and after joining a body of believers, where you can learn the Word, it is our responsibility to grow. Through our prayer life, our personal worship and our intimacy with God, we begin to grow and develop in maturity to be the vessel that is fit for the master's use. We grow and develop in maturity when we allow the dealings of God to work in our lives. This takes more than just church service; it requires our acknowledging God as Lord in every area of our lives. Relationship with God says, He has the authority to rule over your life. It is coming to a place where you recognize that your life is no longer your own. Too many believers get stuck and satisfied with just church service, for the sake of fulfilling a moral obligation. They never get involved out of fear that it will require too much time and accountability.

Religion says that you know there is a God and you know He is good and you know He loves everybody, but you've never tasted for yourself the goodness of God by His Spirit. Religion says I'm OK and it doesn't take all of that! We know that certain things are a sin and we've been taught to have a morally good conscience, so because we don't kill, because we don't steal, because we don't cheat, because we are morally good people, and we mind our business, we are OK. Jesus said, in John 10:10,

"I came to give you life and that life more abundantly."

The only way we will walk in the abundant and overflowing life that Jesus died to give us, will be by our relationship with the Word of God and fellowshipping with the Holy Spirit. It is when we come to a place where we recognize that we are in need of God in our lives. When we begin to humble ourselves under His hand and allow His dealings in our lives, then we will see the fruit of abundance start to spring forth in every area of our lives.

Unlike the children of Israel, they had to follow a specific order that was established by God thru the hand of Moses, in order to have the presence of God dwell among them. The same way God desired to dwell with the children of Israel, He desires to dwell with you and me. Don't become like the hypocrites, confessing that you know God, but your heart being far from Him. Don't just know church service and serve the pastor, and disobey God.

God desires intimacy with you because He longs to bring you into the set place that He has for you. Moses knew the ways of God, the children of Israel only knew the acts of God. (Psalms 103:7) Through your intimacy, you too will become acquainted with the ways of God and the dealings of God in your life. You will see God around you and working through you and in you.

Your Daddy loves you and His desire for you is that you don't stop at church partnership, but you press into the next level of relationship with Him. Psalms 91:1 says,

> ***"He that dwelleth in the secret place of the most High shall abide under the shadow of the Almighty."***
>
> ***(vs 16) "With long life will I satisfy him, and show him my salvation."***

To the person who makes the presence of God and the Word of God their habitation, their dwelling place, their refuge, to that person God said He is gonna show them how good it is to be one of the saved. Child of God, it is a good thing to be saved, but it is better to know the God of your salvation. The same way God raised up Israel and made them into a nation, God desires to raise you up as His very own trophy in the earth.

THE FATHER SEEKETH...

John 4:22-24 says,

"Ye worship ye know not what: we know what we worship: for salvation is of the Jews. But the hour cometh, and now is, when the true worshippers shall worship the Father in spirit and in truth: for the Father Seeketh such to worship him. God is a Spirit: and they that worship him must worship him in spirit and in truth."

What is so interesting about this scripture is that it says the Father seeketh and not God seeketh, indicating relationship. The Greek word for father is "patmos" which means protector, nurturer, provider, upholder. Our God who is the Creator of the Universe is so big, yet so close and personal. He is a Father to the Fatherless and we were created in His image and created for relationship. Psalms 8:4 says,

"What is man that you are mindful of him, the son of man that you care for him?"

Out of all the creations that God created, man was the one He created to be like Him. That alone says so much about who we are in Christ and who we belong to. The Father seeketh true worshippers, not lip service, not form or fashion, but true heartfelt honor and adoration unto the Father.

I'm reminded of a song called "Father Me" and when I heard this song for the first time, I had tears rolling down my face uncontrollably. That song ministered so much to the very core of my soul because, I desired all my life to experience the love of a father. How potent are the words "father me" to the human race. Regardless of how you grew up, male or female, young or old, one parent or two, black or white – deep down inside we all yearn for the love, the nurture and the stability of a father. Well, God said He'll be that to you and through our worship, we allow God to become Father in our lives. It is the Father who desires to love you and comfort you and protect you and cover you and heal you and provide for you. That which you never had, God said He will be that to you. The Father desires to take you in His arms and hold you.

The Father seeketh worshippers who will worship Him in the Spirit. The spirit of man is the part that is just like God. God is a Spirit and it is our spirit that communicates and hears God. We are a spirit, we have a soul and we live in a body. Genesis 1:27 and 2:7 NIV tells us,

"So God created man in his own image, in the image of God he created him; male and female he created them."

"The Lord God formed the man from the dust of the ground and breathed into his nostrils the breath of life and the man became a living being."

God is not going to talk to your flesh nor is He going to talk to your emotions. When we worship God in the spirit, we become naked before God. It's not surface, but when we are open and yielded before the Almighty God, He is able to uncover and mend the broken areas in our lives. Being naked before God, because He is the only One who is able to reach back to the place where the little girl and the little boy were hurt and heal the wounded soul.

There is nothing too hard or too deep or too ugly that your Daddy can't fix when we surrender to Him in worship. That's why, beloved, it's not about going through the motions to appease the flesh, it is honoring and adoring God for who He truly is. It is a heartfelt adoration for a loving God who is the center of everything we do. Our worship unto God says that we recognize His authority and His sovereignty in our lives.

The Father seeketh worshippers who will worship Him in truth. A lot of time, we come before God pretending to be something or someone that we are not. Worshipping the Father in truth also requires us to be naked before God, not being fake or phony but allowing God to show us who we really are.

When we worship God in truth, we allow Him to Father us. We put ourselves in a position to hear from God concerning ourselves and the areas in our lives that need cleansing.

2 Corinthians 7:1 [amp] says,

"Therefore since these [great] promises are ours, beloved, let us cleanse ourselves from everything that contaminates and defiles the body and spirit, and bring [our] consecration to completeness in the [reverential] fear of God."

As we develop a relationship with the Father through our worship, then He will begin to cleanse the filthiness of our flesh and spirit. That is why beloved, as you worship God, open up your heart and allow the pure adoration of your spirit to pour out to your loving Father who is in love with you! Often, the saints are quick to say that there is nothing wrong with them; however, it isn't until

God reveals to us that we are in need of His healing in our lives.

An architect, knowing the construction of a building is aware that the taller the building, the deeper its foundation must be in the ground. The deeper the foundation is what supports the height of the building. It's the same implication in the Kingdom of God. God is our architect and He knows the purpose you were designed to fulfill. Ultimately, as you go deeper into the things of God, through a pure relationship of worship, God will begin to take you higher into the things of the kingdom. Remember, you are already equipped for what you have been designed to fullfil.

Chapter 4

YOU'VE BEEN COMMISSIONED

As believers, we fail to realize that when we received Jesus as Lord of our lives, we didn't just get saved for the sake of escaping hell, but we joined the army of God. The Bible says that we are not to forsake ourselves together with the assembly of the saints. (Hebrews 10:25) Our purpose of going to church isn't just to fulfill an obligation; it is to get equipped in the Word of God, so we might go out and do the work of the ministry. Two scriptures come to mind, that tells us how important the Word of God is to the believer. Titus 1:9 [amp] says,

"He must hold fast to the sure and trustworthy Word of God as he was taught it, so that he may be able both to give stimulating instruction and encouragement in sound (wholesome) doctrine and to refute and convict those who contradict and oppose it [showing the wayward their error]."

2 Timothy 3:16-17 [amp] says,

"Every Scripture is God-breathed (given by His inspiration) and profitable for instruction, for reproof and conviction of sin, for correction of error and discipline in obedience, [and] for training in righteousness (in holy living, in conformity to God's will in thought, purpose and action). So that the man of God may be complete and proficient, well fitted and thoroughly equipped for every good work."

There are no novices in the kingdom of God; we come together as one body to get instructions from the Word so we might go out and do the work that God has commissioned us to do. The Bible says that we might be thoroughly equipped; notice it didn't say equipped. God, who is all-loving and perfect, would never put you on the battlefield ill-prepared. Wherever you are in life right now, know that you are already equipped with everything you need for the assignment at hand.

I'm reminded about a man named Moses, who had absolutely no confidence in himself; but when God called him to fulfill the assignment and task of delivering the children of Israel out of Egypt, God used what he had already. Moses had a staff and God took that, to show forth His power and authority in his life and in the earth. Beloved, it's already inside of you, because God has all the while been effectively working in your life, equipping you for what He has called you to do. (Philippians 2:13 amp) Even when you didn't sense it, He's been getting you ready for the part you are to play in the Kingdom of God.

In the four gospels, we see how the disciples went around with Jesus, listening to his teachings and witnessing his miracles. Faith was being imparted as they walked with Jesus. They were also able to be behind the scene with Jesus in order to get understanding of the parables that Jesus would teach. Ultimately, the disciples were being equipped for what they would soon be doing. Jesus' ministry on earth was for three and a half years, and after his death and resurrection, he handed over the paton to the disciples to finish the race. The church today still has the paton until Jesus comes back to rapture the church, and we are a part of the church. The Bible tells us that we are to occupy until Jesus returns. (Luke 19:13) There is a work that needs to be done and we are the hands, feet, and the mouth of God in the earth, to finish what Jesus started. Jesus said to occupy; that means to do business until He returns.

Jesus came to destroy the works of the devil and in the book of Luke He tells us that we have been given authority to trample over scorpions and all the power of the devil. (Luke 10:19) We have been given the right, the power and the authority to come against every evil work of the devil.

"And he said unto them, Go ye into all the world, and preach the gospel to every creature. He that believeth and is baptized shall be saved; but he that believeth not shall be damned. And these signs shall follow them that believe; In my name shall they cast out devils; they shall speak with new tongues; They shall take up serpents and if they drink any deadly thing, it shall not hurt them, they shall lay hands on the sick and they shall recover."
Mark 16:15-18.

The Bible continues to say that, as they went forth, preaching the Word, the Lord worked with them, confirming the things that came out of their mouths. How awesome to know, that we don't have to do this in our own ability, but the Lord confirms His Word with signs following. Notice that the key word is "His words" not what we think or our opinion, but what thus saith the Lord is what God will confirm with signs following.

Our responsibility is to go forth teaching and sharing our faith, and teaching others to observe the things that we have been taught. Child of God, how will they call on the name of Jesus if they don't believe? And, how will they believe, if they have not heard? And how will they hear without a preacher? And, how will they preach unless they are sent? (Romans 10:14) Beloved, you do not have to have a title to preach this Word, for we have all been commissioned to go out and preach Jesus to a dying world.

People come across your path every day that never make it into a church, to hear the word, and you have enough on the inside of you right now to get started today. Put no confidence in yourself, but trust that the Holy Ghost on the inside of you will bring to remembrance the Word of God and minister through you the love of Christ. Philippians 2:13 [amp] says,

"[Not in your own strength] for it is God who is all the while effectually at work in you [energizing and creating in you the power and desire], both to will and to work for His good pleasure and satisfaction and delight."

We have been created for purpose and we've been given assignment; so, as we grow up into the things of God, He will begin to bring forth the desires of His pleasure through us. We've been commissioned to go forth, tear down, up-root, and to plant seeds into the lives of the people we are assigned to.

You are probably saying, "Who am I assigned to?" How do I tear down or up-root? Trust me; if you have accepted Jesus Christ as Lord, you are assigned to somebody and you start through prayer. Interceding on behalf of those who are hurting, and for those who you are assigned to, is where you start in your assignment. As you pray for others, you will begin to see doors open that will allow you to share God's Word.

God is waiting for us to take the first step so we can be instruments in His hand and for His glory in the lives of God's people. You have something on the inside of you right now that is going to be a tremendous blessing to someone who is going to come across your path. Evangelist, Teachers, Pastors, Apostles, and Prophets are not assigned to everybody; they've been commanded to perfect the saints, for the work of the ministry and the edifying of the body of Christ. (Ephesians 4:11-12) Once again, their role is to perfect you, so that you might be complete for the work of the ministry. There is a work that must be done and it's going to be done by your hands.

    I have a storefront where I run a graphic design, printing and publishing business. I get a lot of business and a lot of traffic comes through my doors. I always pray for the people that I am assigned to. I don't know who they are; but, my prayer is that God would give me wisdom, counsel and revelation pertaining to the deliverance, healing and salvation of His people.

    By me praying for those I am assigned to, I become more sensitive to the leadership of Holy Spirit, when people come across my path. I have so many testimonies of doors that were opened and how I said one word that led me into ministering. I have had people tell me that I was on it, or how they needed to hear that or how I just confirmed what was already in them. I have had people crying in my shop or just be in a daze, because I spoke a NOW Word for them. They came in my shop for one reason; but, they walked into the anointing and they received much more than what they came in for. So many people are in a place of deliberation and need to hear a Word of direction and get clarity from God. Many people have told me that after I minister or pray, its like a BIG LOAD or WEIGHT lifted off their shoulders.

    I believe that I am effective, because I pray for those I am assigned to and in prayer I've already released the answers to their needs. It was God working in me and through me to meet the needs of His people. We are vessels and instruments in the earth that God uses in order that His glory can be seen. Remember, you've been commissioned and God is waiting for you. It's time that we grow up and allow His character and power to be perfected in us.

JESUS, OUR EXAMPLE

Philippians 2:6,7 (amp) says,

"Who, although being essentially one with God and in the form of God [possessing the fullness of the attributes which make God God], did not think this equality with God was a thing to be eagerly grasped or retained. But stripped Himself [of all privileges and rightful dignity], so as to assume the guise of a servant (slave), in that He became like men and was born a human being."

Jesus came down from heaven, stripped from His royalties, born of a virgin and made into the likeness of man so that He might be our example of a servant in the earth. The Bible tells us about the accounts surrounding the birth of Jesus (Matthew 1 and 2) as well as an account of him at 12 yrs old in the temple. (Luke 2:41-51) It's not until Jesus was 30 years old that He steps onto the scene to start His public ministry. In the early years of Jesus or, should I say the silent years of ministry, the Bible says that Jesus grew in wisdom, stature and favor with God and man. (Luke 2:52) It also says that Jesus waxed strong in the spirit. (Luke 2:40) Even though Jesus was the son of God, He was also the son of man and He set the example of one who spent time with God and learned of the teachings, in the synagogue.

Jesus went to church and had a one–on-one relationship with the Father. Jesus had a job working with his father as a carpenter, He obeyed His parents and He was learning to obey the laws of the land. When Jesus turned 30 yrs old, He went to the River Jordan and was baptized by John the Baptist, because that was their custom and that is where God confirmed who He was. (Luke 3:21-22) In order for Jesus to be our example in the earth, He couldn't bypass any steps.

The Bible says, God anointed Jesus with the Holy Ghost and power. He went around doing good and healing all those who were sick and oppressed by the devil. (Acts 10:38) Luke tells us that the Spirit of the Lord was on Jesus and he was anointed to heal the broken-hearted, deliver those who were captive and set at liberty all those who were bruised and bound. (Luke 4:18) Jesus didn't do or say anything apart from what He heard His Father say and do. We must remember that Jesus was our example of what a man could do on the earth, when he walked with God and yielded to His Spirit.

God anointed Jesus and He was with Jesus; but, the same way God was with Jesus, God is now with us and has anointed us through and by His Holy Spirit. For the Bible says that the anointing abides in you. (1 John 2:27) Romans 8 tells us that we are heirs of God and joint heirs with Christ and that we received the spirit of adoption because we have been engrafted in. Therefore, the same power, authority and anointing that Jesus walked in is now available to us. That is why Jesus had to come as a man and pave the way for his disciples to carry out their assignments.

Ephesians 2 tells us that we are God's workmanship or handiwork created in Christ Jesus unto good works, which God has pre-ordained that we should walk in. God has pre-arranged and, made ready for us, before we ever stepped on the scene, good works that we should carry out in the earth. God is looking for our availability, not our ability, because it's His anointing, His ability, His power and His grace that will be effectively working through us. That is why Jesus couldn't come as God, but He had to come to our level to redeem us and show us that we too can be mighty men and women in the earth, bringing forth and showing God's glory among men.

The Old Testament saints, the New Testament disciples, and Jesus, were all regular men like you and me; but, when God anointed them for purpose, they became warriors for the Kingdom of God. Jesus also set the example that it was important to get away with God and pray. The Bible continually talked about how Jesus would send the disciples ahead of Him while He went up in the mountain to pray. Jesus would set Himself apart, because He knew the value of spending time with God, and the importance of the anointing being strong on His life, in order to perform the miracles in that day. The more time you spend with God, you allow more of the anointing to flow through your life to produce His power in your life.

Beloved, it is vitally important in this day and time to not just pray on the run, but sit still before the presence of God and allow Him to minister to you. God is the Many-Breasted One and He desires to pour into you all of His nourishment and supply for your life. In other words, sitting in the presence of God produces spiritual power needed in the life of the believer.

The Bible says that Jesus learned obedience through what He suffered. Hebrews 2:10 (amp) says,

"For it was an act worthy [of God] and fitting [to the divine nature] that He for Whose sake and by Whom all things have their existence, in bringing many sons into glory should make the Pioneer of their salvation perfect [should bring to maturity the human experience necessary to be perfectly equipped for His office as High Priest] through suffering."

God was preparing Jesus for His ultimate service and that was to be our High Priest. For we do not have a High Priest that cannot be touched with the feeling of our infirmities, but was in all points tempted like as we are, yet without sin. (Hebrews 4:15) Jesus daily makes intercession on our behalf. There is absolutely nothing going on in your life today or in your past that Jesus can't relate too.

Remember, He came as a man and walked out His purpose on earth because ultimately His greater purpose was to redeem mankind from sin, and break the power of Satan from our lives, pave the way for our salvation, and be the example of a man anointed by God to do the work of the ministry.

AMBASSADORS FOR CHRIST

2 Corinthians 5:20, says

"Now then we are ambassadors for Christ, as though God did beseech you by us: we pray you in Christ's stead, be ye reconciled to God."

The Bible tells us that we are new creatures in Christ, and how we have been given the assignment of reconciling the world back to the Father. God no longer sees us as sinners or wretched undone, but we are the righteousness of God in Christ Jesus. God says that we are ambassadors of Christ. That means we are representatives of the Anointed One and His Anointing. What an honor and privilege to be representatives on earth of this great anointing that is in us. An ambassador is someone who represents, and/or acts on behalf of.

For example, the prime minister of Russia wouldn't come to America, but he would send a representative in his stead. This person would be considered as an ambassador of Russia, because he has been given the authority and power to speak and act on behalf of the Prime Minister. Whatever privileges, rights and immunities that the Prime Minister would have received, now the ambassador has a right to them.

God says that we are His ambassadors on earth to represent the kingdom of Heaven. That is why the Word says that whatever we bind in heaven shall be bound on earth and, whatever we loose in heaven, shall be loosed on earth. (Matthew 18:18) We have been given authority in three worlds. We have been given authority on earth because we were born of a woman. We have been given authority in heaven and underneath the earth because our lives are now hidden in Christ.

Ephesians 2:6 says,

"And hath raised us up together, and made us sit together in heavenly places in Christ Jesus."

Jesus conquered the grave and death when He rose from the dead and our authority comes from being in Him. As an ambassador, we are to be a true representative of what is actually in heaven. Jesus never died for an underground church, He said we are the salt of the earth, the light of the world and a city that sits on a hill that cannot be hid. We are carriers of this anointing and the only way God is going to be seen in the earth, is if it comes from us. We are God's mouthpiece in the earth and we are His chosen generation.

If people are going to hear what God is saying in the earth, it's going to come from His ambassadors. We are His hands and feet in the earth. God is waiting for His ambassadors to stand up to the plate and be the representative that you have been equipped to be. It's already in you. God has already given you His authority and power and might and wisdom to be His ambassadors in the earth.

The Bible says that when Jesus came on the scene, He didn't speak like the scribes (the religious leaders), but He was one that spoke with authority and power that made people pay attention and follow Him. (Luke 4:32) Paul said, that his teaching wasn't with enticing words, but with a demonstration of God's power and anointing. (1 Corinthians 2:4) It's time that we walk in our rightful positions as ambassadors and also walk in the things that Jesus died to give us.

Ambassadors, who are exercising God's power in our lives and being a voice in the land that Jesus still heals and delivers. We are to command demons of oppression to back up off of people's minds, for we are the voice of God in the earth. God is waiting for you! Everything you need to walk in your calling as an ambassador is already in you. Start where you are and watch God enlarge you. As an ambassador, we are to proclaim God's truth against every lie of the devil. We are the light of the world, but if we don't allow God to shine though us, how will those know that they are in darkness.

Isaiah 60:1 says,

"Arise and shine for the glory of the Lord is risen up on you."

That means to change your position, your posture, and change your countenance for the glory of God's grace and power is risen up on you for the world to see His goodness, His power and His ability in you, on you and around you. Child of God, it is time that we become the voice that crieth in the wilderness, clearing away every obstacle and making straight and smooth the way of the Lord so that His glory and majesty and splendor will be revealed among all flesh to see. (Isaiah 40:3-5 amp)

Chapter 5

EVIL IS PRESENT

The 24th chapter of Matthew talks about the signs surrounding the end of the age and what we should expect to see that would let us know that the end was soon.

"And Jesus answered and said unto them, take heed that no man deceive you. For many shall come in my name, saying I am Christ and shall deceive many. And ye shall hear of wars and rumors of wars, see that ye be not troubled, for all these things must come to pass, but the end is not yet. For nations shall rise against nations and kingdom against kingdom and there shall be famines and pestilences and earthquakes in divers places. All these are the beginning of sorrows. And many false prophets shall rise and shall deceive many. And because iniquity shall abound the love of many shall wax cold. But he that shall endure unto the end, the same shall be saved. And this gospel of the kingdom shall be preached in all the world for a witness unto all nations and then shall the end come."
Matthew 24:4-8; 11-14

Evil has always been present. Let's look back at the beginning of time, after the fall of Adam and Eve. Evil caused Cain to kill his only brother, Abel, because of jealousy. (Genesis 4:8) In the book of Genesis, God saw that the wickedness of man was so great, and that every imagination of the thoughts of their hearts was evil. At that moment, the Lord repented and was grieved in His heart that He ever made man. (Genesis 6:5-6) Even after God brought the flood and started over with one man by the name of Noah, man continued to do evil in the sight of God.

God made covenant with a man named Abram, which later became Abraham and said that he would be the father of many nations. God would make him exceedingly fruitful and God would make nations of thee and kings would come out of him. This covenant would be established between God and Abraham's seed after thee in their generation for an everlasting covenant. They would be God's people and God would be their God and that God would bring them into a land that was flowing with milk and honey as their inheritance. (Genesis 17:1-8) Even 25 years after the covenant was established, God was faithful to Abraham when he begot Isaac and Isaac begot Jacob (Israel) and out of Jacob's seed came the children of Israel.

The children of Israel were God's chosen people that He made into a nation and chose to demonstrate His power through. They had a reputation among the other nations that God was with them. They were not mighty in number or their demeanor, but they were mighty in God's strength and their reputation preceded them. Time after time, day after day, God demonstrated that He was God and that there was no other God beside Him. God demonstrated to them that He was not limited by natural or physical limitations, but that He was able to deliver them, provide for them and protect them. God demonstrated that He would provide their food, substance and water in the midst of their wilderness. He demonstrated that He was able to keep them, sustain them, make a way of escape for them and be a strong tower to them. Even though God continually demonstrated His love toward them and delivered other nations into their hands, without a leader in front of them, the children of Israel continually did evil in the sight of God.

The Bible said in the book of Judges that, after Joshua died, a new generation arose that didn't know the Lord or the works that He had done; therefore, they did evil in the sight of the Lord and served Baalim. Nevertheless, the Lord raised up judges, kings and prophets which delivered them out of the hand of those that spoiled them. (Judges 2:16) Because Israel didn't obey God fully by driving out all the inhabitants of the land, those other nations became a thorn in their side and their god became a snare unto them. The things that the children of Israel saw the other nations do, they started entertaining those same customs. The children of Israel were sacrificing their children, they would make images of gods that were of Baal and they would do as they were doing, which was evil in the sight of the Lord.

God's love never left the children of Israel, but when they did evil, God allowed the other nations to conquer the children of Israel. When the children of Israel would repent, then God would cause them to prevail against their adversary. God needed to show the children of Israel that they were nothing without Him and how it was His power, might and strength that rested on their lives, causing them to be great in the earth. All throughout the Old Testament, we see that God was committed to the covenant that He made with Abraham and that He would be their God, and they would be His people, in spite of their actions.

We also see that all throughout the Old Testament that the children of Israel did evil, and there were kings that did evil in the sight of the Lord. In Jesus' day, there were evil religious leaders who also didn't know God, but they were hard taskmasters to God's people. They were hypocrites and God didn't like that, because they would say one thing, and do another. They would oppress God's people with high taxes on their belongings. Evil is what caused Judas to betray Jesus for 30 pieces of silver. Evil caused religious leaders to let loose a thief and a killer in exchange for Jesus' crucifixion. A person who only went about doing good, healing the sick and setting the oppressed free. Evil is what caused the religious leaders to whip, mock, spit on, crown with thorns, nail to the cross and then kill Jesus.

Child of God, evil has always been present on the earth, so what makes the scripture in Matthew 24 any different from what we have been seeing all along. Jesus, knowing within Himself that His time on the earth was drawing nigh, that is why they couldn't throw Him off the cliff or kill Him before time, because He said my time is not yet. Jesus said that no one takes His life, but He freely gives His life. He could have called forth a legion of angels to deliver Him, but He chose to die for me and for you. That's the power of love. So, the first time Jesus came to the earth was to establish the Kingdom of God and redeem God's people back to Himself. Jesus also lets us know that He is coming back again, but this time, to bring the church (the ones who made Jesus Christ their Lord and Savior, the one's who have been washed in the blood of Jesus) back unto the Father that we might reign with Him forever. (1 Thessalonians 4:13-18)

Jesus prepares us by letting us know that we are going to hear about wars and rumors of wars. Gross darkness will be seen on the earth, violence and devastation, earthquakes and other natural disasters shall be seen at greater levels on the earth, but the time still isn't yet. Matthew 24 is equivalent to birth pains that a woman goes through when she is in labor to have a baby. As a woman is in labor, the closer she gets to actually giving birth to her

Evil Is Present

child, her pains intensify and become sharper and more frequent, her womb begins to expand to bring forth what is on the inside of her. Her body goes through changes so it might prepare for the birthing of the baby and sometimes the changes you experience bring discomfort and pain. Jesus is letting the church know that what we read in Matthew 24, will start to become more frequent, because the earth will experience the labor pains in order to give way and bring forth the second coming of our Lord Jesus Christ.

The news is filled with disaster, violence, murder, and other hideous things that are happening on the earth. Just in the last several years, we have had reports of terrorism attacks, the tremendous terror of 9-11, which is the episode where terrorist crashed several airplanes into the Pentagon in Washington, DC and the New York Trade Center. More intense level hurricanes and tornados back -to-back than we have ever had, Tsunami which was the wall of water that came up out of the coast and killed hundreds of thousands of people in India, gas prices higher than they have ever been, outbreaks of bird flu and diseases that were airborne, scares with our meats being infected, and sniper attacks.

The news also reports that, in some states, they have signed a law that same sex marriage is legal, more reports of kids killing their parents and the entertainment industry has more movies that have religious and demonic under tones. The ultimate news report is that society is beginning to implement a procedure where they are putting chips under the skin of humans and using dogs to locate them. In some states, this is already legal.

Jesus said, when we see the intensity of more and more things happening in the earth back-to-back, then know that the end is soon. No man knows the exact day or time, but God will allow us to know the season.

Jesus shares in Matthew 25, about the parable of the ten virgins. Five virgins were wise because they took their lamps and had oil with them. But, the five foolish virgins weren't prepared because they didn't have any oil for their lamps. Jesus says in verse 13, that we are to:

> *"watch therefore, for ye know neither the day nor the hour wherein the Son of man cometh."*

Jesus admonishes us to be alert, be aware and be ready. We are not to be like the foolish virgins who thought they had a lot of time to get ready. We must be ready and be quick to adapt into the places where God is taking us.

The Word of God was given to us for reproof, corrections and instructions, in righteousness (2 Timothy 3:16). Everything you need pertaining to life and godliness, God said He has already given to you, for it is in His Word. (2 Peter 1:3) As evil presents itself all around you, you must know that God has already made a way of escape for you. (1 Corinthians 10:13) God's Word serves as our refuge, which is a place of safety for you as you dwell and abide in Him. In spite of the news reports, know that God is well able to keep you and sustain you in the midst of any situation.

Watch and pray means to be observant to the changes that are taking place around you and abide in His presence through prayer that your love won't grow cold because of what's going on in the earth. Beloved, fear not because God's Word says we win! Yes, I said it, as believers we are all winners in Christ. The Bible tells us that we overcome by the blood of the lamb and the word of our testimony. That means we overcome every obstacle, every situation, every dilemma even the world's crisis, through the Word of God. The Bible also tells us that Jesus has already overcome the world, so fret not, for the workers of iniquity soon shall be cut off. That's our covenant and that's a promise that we can take to the bank.

Hallelujah! Even though evil is present, at the same time, God's power will begin to be seen in the lives of His people in a greater measure.

must endure the temporary discomfort that goes along with the process of getting to the permanent blessing

Chapter 6

END TIME HARVEST

I've heard preachers say for years that we were living in the last days and Jesus was soon to return. Even as I listen to tapes dated in the late 80's, preachers have always been declaring that these are the last days. Well, the Bible says, that no one knows the day or the hour when Jesus shall return, but we do know that He is coming back for His own. (Matthew 25:13) The ones who have confessed Jesus as Lord and been washed in His blood, those are the ones that Jesus will call unto Himself. (1 Thessalonians 4:16) However, before Jesus returns, we can be assured, that we will see manifestations of harvest that will be gathered in this end time. In the previous chapter, we talked about devastations that will take place before the return of the Lord. In this chapter, I want to focus on the church and what we can expect to see before the return of the Lord.

The word "harvest" is defined as the time of the year when grain, fruit, etc. are gathered in; the gathering in of any crop; the outcome of any effort. The end time harvest will be the display or the gathering of the greatest outpouring of God's glory that has ever been displayed on earth. The book of Acts, chapter 2, echoes what the prophet Joel prophesied would take place in the last days. Peter prophesied that, in the last days, God would pour out His spirit upon all flesh. (Acts 2:17-20) What God was saying was that it is coming a day that He was going to show Himself off in the earth through all men, young or old and regardless of their status or titles. There would be signs and wonders that shall be demonstrated in the earth. Signs and wonders are events that are sovereign manifestations of strange events that would be classified as "attention getters". The purpose of signs and wonders is so people would acknowledge and fully believe that God is God. That there is none other like our God and that He reigns forever.

You are probably thinking, like so many people I have heard say, "we don't see God's demonstrations and miracles like they saw it in the Bible days." Child of God, the Bible says that in the last days we shall see a mighty outpouring of God's glory and power and miracles on the earth. Haggai 2:9 says,

"The glory of this latter house shall be greater than of the former, saith the Lord of hosts; and in this place will I give peace, saith the Lord of host."

God says that His manifested presence, which is the glory, shall be seen at a greater measure than we have ever seen or heard or read about before. Although the world may be experiencing chaos, God's promise to the ones, who are walking with Him, is that in your set place, He will give you peace. Child of God, you were created for such a time as this that you might be used by God to shake your generation for the glory of God. All things that God put in your hands are possible. For it's never too late, regardless of how old you are and where you've been – it's not too late. We are living in the time of harvest, the time of breakthrough, the time of greatness and power that shall be demonstrated for all man to see. Regardless of what you have been through in your past or your experiences, set backs, or disappointments etc., God says your latter shall be greater than your past. Hallelujah! That is a covenant that your Awesome Father made with you before you were born.

Isaiah 2:2,3 says,

"And it shall come to pass in the last days, that the mountain of the Lord's house shall be established in the top of the mountains and shall be exalted above the hills; and all the nations shall flow unto it. And many people shall go and say, come ye, and let us go up to the mountain of the Lord to the house of the God of Jacob; and he will teach us of his ways, and we will walk in his paths; for out of Zion shall go forth the law and the word of the Lord from Jerusalem."

Child of God, the Bible says out of the mouths of two or three witnesses let every word be established. Isaiah backs up what we read in Haggai as it relates to what God would do in the earth during the end time harvest. We need to know that, as we approach this season of the end time harvest, the Lord's house and His kingdom, shall be established above everything that society has exalted in the earth. I said it before and it stands repeating, Jesus never died for an underground church, or a church without power or victory, for we are a city on the hill that cannot be hid.

Over the generations, the gospel has been watered down, we've picked and chose what we were going to preach about; we've declared what was for now and what had passed away. So, because we as leaders, have not proclaimed the entire gospel, we have not seen the entire covenant manifested. But in this end time harvest, God is raising up a new breed, a new generation that will dare to trust God and step out on His spoken Word, trusting that He is God and He would do all that He said He would do. God said that He would take the foolish and weak things and confound the wise and mighty. (1 Corinthians 2) It's not about how inadequate you feel or about what you think you lack, child of God, know that if God said it, He will bring it to pass and walk you through every step. Verse 3 in Isaiah 2, talks about how people will begin to come into the church, to be taught the ways of God and to learn how to walk in the path of our God. There will be something different and distinct about the body where many will see. No longer shall the church look like the world, but God would begin to exalt and lift up the church in a demonstration of his power and grace.

The only way the church will begin to rise in this power, is through an abiding relationship and trust in God as they step out into the unknown, the unfamiliar and the uncomfortable. God's promise to us is that as He leads us into places we've never been before, He will make darkness light before us. That means He will begin to illuminate our mind to what we need to know as we are in route. As you step out on God, not knowing everything, He would begin to give you clarity when you need it. He daily will provide for the journey. He will also make the crooked places straight. That means, He is responsible for clearing away the obstacles. These things will He do and not forsake us. (Isaiah 42:16)

I'm reminded about Esther, who God used to bring deliverance and enlargement to the Jews in her generation. She declared, that if I perish, I perish, but who knows if I haven't been raised up for such a time as this. As a result, God stretched forth His hand and brought deliverance in a mighty way and exalted Esther in the process.

In Isaiah 60:1-5, God says to arise and shine. Arise from that place of depression and/or that place of prostration in which circumstances have kept you down. Arise to a new way of living and to a new life in Him, for old things have passed away and

End Time Harvest

everything has become new. Arise to a new way of thinking and expand your capacity to believe God for more. God says that His glory has come; His heavy laden manifested presence has risen up on you where others will see. The Bible says that darkness will be upon the earth and gross darkness upon the people. What that means is that the morale of society, as a whole, will become dim. They will begin to see that which is wrong as now being right in their eyes. We will begin to see more disasters and reports of grievous crimes that were never heard of before, because the signs of the times are pointing to this being the last days. But, as we behold His promises, God says that even though darkness will be upon the earth, His glory will be seen on His people.

Different ethnic groups, people in leadership, people of honorable status, even the government will begin to run to the light. At one time, society turned to its own wisdom and its own ability and even the government. The Bible says that the government will be upon the shoulders of the church. (Isaiah 9:6) There is coming a day, that all man will see God's power and splendor on the earth and it's going to be seen through the people of God, the church that God is going to raise up and exalt in the earth.

Look up my brethren, and look around you for the Bible says that people will begin to flock to the people of God for answers and help and deliverance. No longer shall the church be underground or void of power, like the world, but we hold the true answers. This will only happen as you allow the Almighty God to penetrate your heart and mold you into the vessel that is meat for the Master's use. God is waiting on you beloved, for the kings scepter is extended. He is beckoning you to come into Him so He can use you in this end time harvest that awaits the expecting. Isaiah 66 says, that He will not bring you to the place and time of giving birth to the promises and to all that lies on the inside of you and then not bring it forth. The scripture says, that after the children of Zion travailed, then they brought forth.   (Isaiah 66:7-9)

Child of God, regardless of what it looks like and what seems to be taking place around you, DON'T ABORT THE PROCESS. Keep on praying and keep on worshiping because we are living in the greatest time in history. God is raising His people up as world changers and history makers to usher in the greatest outpouring of His anointing and power that we have ever seen.

Joel 2:23-27 says,

"… for he has given you the former rain moderately, and he will cause to come down for you the rain, the former rain and the latter rain in the first month. And the floors shall be full of wheat and the vats shall overflow with wine and oil. … and ye shall know that I am in the midst of Israel, and that I am the lord your God and none else; and my people shall never be ashamed."

Beloved, when God said He would give us rain, He was saying that He was going to give us what was needed in order to increase and produce what is in our hands. The former rain was to prepare the soil for the seed that shall be deposited in it. The latter rain was a steady and continuous rain that penetrated the soil to break open the shell of the seed in the ground when planted. So the life force in that seed would break forth out of the shell that it is contained in.

There is coming a day when God will pour out both rains in the same month. That means He will combine the sowing of the former rain and the reaping of the latter rain, so you will experience the double portion rain power of God. Once again, DON'T ABORT THE PROCESS, God is positioning His people to experience the greatest outpouring of God's power and miracle in the earth. God loves you and He wants the best for you. He knows your destiny, and your full potential. He knows what you are made of. He's not intimidated by your past failures. He knows how to bring you into your destiny. Let Him! As you step out to trust God to lead you, I promise that you won't regret being in the Master's loving hand. He's faithful to all those who love Him.

NOT ONE
WORD FROM GOD
IS WITHOUT
POWER
OR IMPOSSIBLE
OF
FULFILLMENT

Chapter 7

THE TESTIMONY

Finally, my friend, let me share my testimony with you. I was one who, skidded out of high school, never went to college and have been in the secretarial field my entire working career. I never thought I could do anything else outside the secretarial or customer service field. I married the first guy who came along because I never had good relationships. I went from man to man like I went from job to job. I was always in search for something, but never finding it. I was void of vision, purpose and goals, not realizing that I was going in circles. After three years of marriage, I got divorce and moved back home with my mother, because I never thought I could make it on my own. Often times I felt like a failure and a disappointment, because I never felt within myself that I had accomplished anything.

One day in the summer of 2002, God birthed a graphic design and printing business in me. No prior experience or training, God anointed me not only to do graphics, but gave me the ability to run the many facets of a business. I incorporated my business in January 2003, and by the time September 2003 came around, God moved me out of my mother's house and said "He was going to grow me up." Around the same time, God showed me who my mate was and said "You will not walk with him the way you normally would, but you would come into Me and hear from Me." At that moment, I knew my journey had just shifted and God was taking me to the next level of faith.

December 2003, God said, "to make this school year my last school year on that job." I was gung ho until people who saw my financials said "to pay off your bills and put some money in the bank." All that made sense to me, so my goal was to save some money. Well, when the next school year started, I was still there. How many know that what God said, He meant. So in August 2004, God showed me a vision that I was coming off my job, and I told God, that I was going to come off next year because I didn't save any money and I still had bills. September 2004, there was a prophetic word that came forth at my church that said, "some of you have your own business and God has been trying to get you off your job and how much money you are missing by staying on your job, now LEAP, because if you don't, you will always reason why you need to stay." The Spirit of God was all over me, but in my mind it made no sense for me to quit, because I didn't live at home with my mother anymore and I had bills.

So I started praying everyday, "God show me how to come off my job" and two weeks later, God showed me a vision that I was going to be fired for something that I didn't do. I cried in the presence of God and said, "I didn't want to go out like that." God said, "I gave you three opportunities to leave and you would not." Two days later, (not two months, not two years, but two DAYS) October 8, 2004, I got fired for something I didn't do. Then, I was denied unemployment and the printer, where I was working one hour a day, could not pay me any more money because he was just making it. At that moment, God said, "I will shut every door and let you know that I am providing for you, now sow into that man's business and I will cause you to reap in yours." I started working five hours every day and the printer still paid me like I was working one hour a day. Two months later, December 2004, God said, "now go and get your own place."

By this time, I am on the floor screaming, but I knew I had to keep walking this out. It was tight going forward, but I had no where to turn back. I went through the motion of looking for a place, for a print shop that I had no furniture and no equipment for. In route to somewhere else, I did a double take at this building and I heard God say, "That's it!" I instantly had supernatural favor with the owner of the building. The down payment to move in came from a mutual fund that I had forgotten about. Then, I wanted to get a loan because common sense says, when you move in somewhere you were going to need things, but God said "No!" So, when I moved in, everything in my building was given to me and the owner paid my first three months of utilities. Supernatural Favor!

With every level that God was taking me, I had to step into the next level before I saw the provision and favor of that next level. All I kept hearing from God throughout this entire process was, "when you can leave what you see, for what you hear, there is a multitude of blessings on the other side." God would say, "so many people are waiting for things to line up before they step," He said "Karen you will never see it until you step." Because I dared to step out and trust God, He tripled my business the first year I was in the building. I went from doing a little over 36K in sales to over 117K in sales. Then God increased my sales the following year an additional 35%. Remember, my business never reflected it could take care of me, when I was laid off from my job, but it wasn't until I got into the place that God needed me, that I saw the provision of God.

My business is not just a business, but a ministry, because God has afforded me the opportunity to minister to and pray for so many people who have come in and out of my building. I have witnessed countless of times that people came in for business and came in contact with the anointing on my life; that caused impact in their lives. I am a vessel and an instrument that God uses on an ongoing basis to cause lives to be changed. God is using my testimony to empower others to walk into their destiny. But the story doesn't stop here.

In June 2006, God birthed my second company called Daughters of Zion Empowerment Center, Inc., where I am the founder and president of a non-profit, Christian outreach ministry providing services to women who are secretly hurting. Then, in August 2006, God birthed my third company called Anointed Press Publishers. I originally opened this company to publish my own book, but He has already sent me customers, within the first month, for me to publish their books.

I often tell God that He is moving a little too fast. But, remember He knows the true potential that lies in us and it is our job to keep up with God. Our confidence must rest in knowing that God would never open a door that we were not ready for. So, even though our minds are telling us that we're not ready, we have to trust God and keep walking it out. He is bringing us into the fullness of our destinies.

God has raised me up as a living testimony of the power and grace of the Almighty God and how He is able to do exceedingly and abundantly above all we ask or think and it's all for the glory of God. Child of God, step out on what God is speaking to you and watch Him do the supernatural in your life, for this is the time of harvesting and we will see the greatest outpouring, of God's miracles and glory we have ever seen.

A friend once shared with me something very profound,

"The level of our thinking, acting and operating that got you to where you are right now – will not take you to where it is that God wants you to be." That tremendously blessed me. To me it meant that no matter where I was in my life and no matter what I had accomplished, I still had to stay in the presence of God and allow Him to transform me. Transform my thinking, transform how I saw and responded to situations, transform how I even saw myself, in order to reach my full potential in God. In order to reach the height that God ordained for the church to accomplish, we need to know that there will always be seasons of changing, developing, pruning, and re-defining of self in the presence of the Lord. And its after that season, comes the next level of increase springing forth in your life.

God is waiting on **YOU**! Let Him put you on that next level of faith journey, that will ultimately catapult you into your next level of glory.

YOU ARE POSITIONED FOR GOD'S MIRACLE

Romans 10:9,10 says,

"That if thou confess with thou mouth the Lord Jesus and believe in your heart that He is risen from the dead you shall be saved. For with the heart man believeth unto righteousness and the with mouth confession is made unto salvation."

If you have never confessed Jesus as Lord of your life or you want to re-dedicate your life back to Christ, please say the following prayer.

A Prayer of Salvation

Open your mouth and say aloud… "Jesus I believe that you died and rose from the dead on my behalf as my eternal sacrifice. I repent of my sins and I ask that you forgive me and cleanse me of all unrighteousness. I ask that you come into my heart and abide in me. I make you Lord of my life and I thank you for saving me now.

Congratulations!

You are now part of the family of God. If you do not have a church home, pray and ask God to direct you to a church that is teaching the word so you can begin to walk out the desires and potential that God placed on the inside of you.

ABOUT THE AUTHOR

Minister Karen is the Founder & President of Anointed Press Graphics, Inc., birthed in 2002, Anointed Press Publishers and Daughters of Zion Empowerment Center, Inc., birthed in 2006.

Minister Karen, a native Washingtonian, chosen in the midst of this generation and ordained by God, was called into the ministry in 1995. In 1998, she was licensed as a minister under Spirit of Faith Christian Center, led by Senior Pastors Drs. Michael and Dee Dee Freeman, where she continues to serve and worship. During the silent years of ministry, God saw fit to release Minister Karen to coordinate a home-based bible study for over 5 years. This mission represents the cornerstone of her ministry. It has allowed her to embrace and joyously share her passion to enlighten the people of God about the teachings of Christ. Minister Karen serves as counselor, mentor, and teacher to many individuals, who have crossed her path, that she has gracefully embraced. She is regarded by many as a caring and compassionate disciple and has effectively impacted the lives of people she has served.

Minister Karen's heart-centered love for God has inspired individuals to develop an intimate relationship with God throughout the body of Christ. She focuses on exhorting the body of

Christ to live with spiritual integrity and fullness as they embrace their inheritance as Christian believers. Her ministry stands to light the way out of pain and sorrow for many women, encouraging them that God can heal even the broken- hearted.

God has raised up Minister Karen in this 21st century to usher the body of Christ into the greatest outpouring of God's glory in the end time harvest. A strong anointing rest in her while signs and wonders follow her ministry. God has empowered her voice as a weapon against the kingdom of darkness as she shares her gifts throughout the body of Christ.

Minister Karen's vision is to empower others to trust and lean on God for He can take you from nothing to being a living testimony for Him.

TO CONTACT THE AUTHOR:

Karen M. Presley
c/o Anointed Press Graphics
11191 Crain Highway
Cheltenham, Maryland 20623
301-782-2285

Monday - Friday
10:00 a.m. - 6:00 p.m.

Please include your testimony or help received from this book when you write.

Your prayer requests are also welcomed.

TO ORDER MORE BOOKS:

www.anointedpresspublishers.com

Daughters of Zion Empowerment Center

Daughters of Zion Empowerment Center (DZEC) is a 501 (c)(3) non-denominational, multi-cultural, nonprofit Christian outreach ministry providing services to women who are secretly hurting.

The core purpose/mission of DZEC is to empower women through the Word of God, by creating avenues of hope for those who are broken, bruised and secretly hurting; enabling them to see that there is a way out. DZEC stands to pave the way for women who are experiencing pain and sorrow, assuring them that God can heal even the broken-hearted.

Your generous donation to DZEC will enable us to make a difference in the lives of many women. We are priviledge to be co-laborers with God in changing lives and making a difference.

With your help, we can do this.

Please consider sowing a monthly donation and/or becoming a volunteer to support the vision of DZEC.

Visit our website to find out more about the ministry.

www.dzec.org

Living Holy in an Unholy World
ORDER FORM

Use this convenient order form to order
Living Holy in an Unholy World

Please Print:

NAME: _____

ADDRESS: _____

CITY: _____ STATE: _____

ZIP: _____

PHONE: _____ CELL: _____

_____ copies of Book @ $10.00 each $_____
_____ copies of Journal @ $10.00 each $_____
_____ copies of Book & Journal @ $17.00 each $_____
(If you live in the State of Maryland) 5% tax $_____
Postage and handling @ $3.00 per book $_____
Total amount enclosed $_____

Make checks payable to ***Anointed Press Publishers***

Send to:
Anointed Press Publishers
11191 Crain Highway
Cheltenham, MD 20623